AMERICA

THE ERA OF TRANSFORMATION

PRATAP SINGH

Contents

Preface

America- An Era Of Revolution meant for all classes and all people is a part of "History" with Geography book brought out seperately.

In the modern context, history education deals with concepts , processes, applications , creativity and world view.

History also regarded as study of past is perhaps the mmost fascinating of all subjects and is very relevant in the lives of people --- in terms of knowledge about past, answering the question who, why , when, what and how.

--------- Samrat Pratap Singh

Acknowledgements

I would like to express my special thanks of gratitude to my history teacher Mrs Baneerjee for their able guidance and support in completing my book.

I would also like to extend my gratitude to my parents for providing me with all the facilities .

Samrat Pratap Singh

CHAPTER ONE

What Was The American Revolution

The American Revolution—also called the U.S. War of Independence—was the insurrection fought between 1775 and 1783 through which 13 of Great Britain's North American colonies threw off British rule to establish the sovereign United States of America, founded with the Declaration of Independence in 1776.

CHAPTER TWO

Origin Of American Revolution

By 1774, the year leading up to the Revolutionary War, trouble was brewing in America. Parliament (England's Congress) had been passing laws placing taxes on the colonists in America. There had been the Sugar Act in 1764, the Stamp Act the following year, and a variety of other laws that were meant to get money from the colonists for Great Britain. The colonists did not like these laws.

Great Britain was passing these laws because of the French and Indian War, which had ended in 1763. That war, which had been fought in North America, left Great Britain with a huge debt that had to be paid. Parliament said it had fought the long and costly war to protect its American subjects from the powerful French in Canada. Parliament said it was right to tax the American colonists to help pay the bills for the war.

Most Americans disagreed. They believed that England had fought the expensive war mostly to strengthen its empire and increase its wealth, not to benefit its American subjects. Also, Parliament was elected by people living in England, and the colonists felt that lawmakers living in England could not understand the colonists' needs. The colonists felt that since they did not take part in voting for members of Parliament in England they were not represented in Parliament. So Parliament did not have the right to take their money by imposing taxes. "No taxation without representation" became the American rallying cry.

In 1774 much of this unrest had calmed down, especially in the southern colonies. Most North Carolinians carried on their daily lives on farms raising crops and tending herds, and in cities shopkeeping, cooking, sewing, and performing dozens of other occupations and tasks. They did not often think about the king of England or his royal governor in North Carolina.

But beneath this calm surface there were problems. Just three years earlier at Great Alamance Creek, 2,000 Tar Heel farmers called Regulators had led an uprising, the largest armed rebellion in any English colony to that time. They wanted to "regulate" the governor's corrupt local officials, who were charging huge fees and seizing property. The royal governor, William Tryon, and his militia crushed the rebellion at the Battle of Alamance.

Another problem beneath the surface calm lay with the large African and American Indian populations. Many in these two groups hated their low positions in a society dominated by powerful whites. Some white colonists believed that if a war with England broke out, these other Tar Heels would support the king in hopes of gaining more control over their own lives.

Finally, Tar Heels knew that other colonies were continuing to resist English control. In 1773, colonists in Boston, Massachusetts, had thrown shipments of tea into the harbor rather than pay Parliament's taxes on the tea. The Boston Tea Party aroused all the colonies against Parliament, which was continuing to show its scorn for the colonists' welfare.

The movement against English rule spread rapidly. In April 1775 British soldiers, called lobsterbacks because of their red coats, and minutemen—the colonists' militia—exchanged gunfire at Lexington and Concord in Massachusetts. Described as "the shot heard round the world," it signaled the start of the American Revolution and led to the creation of a new nation.

North Carolina joined the war the following month. In New Bern on May 23, Abner Nash (who later became governor) led a group of Whigs to Tryon Palace to seize the cannon there. Eight days later, Governor Martin became the first royal governor in the colonies to flee office. He sought refuge in Fort Johnston at the mouth of the Cape Fear River. In July he had to leave the fort and fled to the safety of a British ship anchored offshore.

For eight years the Old North State was the scene of suffering caused by the war for independence. There were battles and bloodshed: the Battle of Moore's Creek Bridge in February 1776, the destruction that summer of the Cherokee Indian villages in western North Carolina by Patriot leader Griffith Rutherford, and the battles at Kings Mountain and Guilford Courthouse. There were deaths and injuries, terrible shortages of food and warm clothing, destruction and loss of property, and constant fear.

CHAPTER THREE

Major Causes Of Revolution

The Stamp Act (March 1765)

On February 6th, 1765 George Grenville rose in Parliament to offer the fifty-five resolutions of his Stamp Bill. A motion was offered to first read petitions from the Virginia colony and others was denied. The bill was passed on February 17, approved by the Lords on March 8th, and two weeks later ordered in effect by the King. The Stamp Act was Parliament's first serious attempt to assert governmental authority over the colonies. Great Britain was faced with a massive national debt following the Seven Years War. That debt had grown from £72,289,673 in 1755 to £129,586,789 in 1764*. English citizens in Britain were taxed at a rate that created a serious threat of revolt.

AN ACT for granting and applying certain stamp duties, and other duties, in the British colonies and plantations in America, towards further defraying the expenses of defending, protecting, and securing the same; and for amending such parts of the several acts of parliament relating to the trade and revenues of the said colonies and plantations, as direct the manner of determining and recovering the penalties and forfeitures therein mentioned.

WHEREAS, by an act made in the last session of Parliament several duties were granted, continued, and appropriated toward defraying the expenses of defending, protecting, and securing the British colonies and plantations in America; and whereas it is just and necessary that provision be made for raising a further revenue within your majesty's dominions in America toward defraying the said expenses; we, your majesty's most dutiful and loyal subjects, the Commons of Great Britain, in Parliament assembled, have therefore resolved to give and grant unto your majesty the several rates and duties hereinafter mentioned; and do humbly beseech your majesty that it may be enacted, and be it enacted by the king's most excellent majesty, by and with the advice and consent of the lords spiritual and temporal, and commons, in this present Parliament assembled, and by the authority of the same, that from and after the first day of November, one thousand seven hundred and sixty five, there shall be raised, levied, collected, and paid unto his majesty, his heirs, and successors, throughout the colonies and plantations in America, which now are, or hereafter may be, under the dominion of his majesty, his heirs and successors:

For every skin or piece of vellum or parchment, or sheet or piece of paper, on which shall be engrossed, written, or printed, any declaration, plea, replication, rejoinder, demurrer or other pleading, or any copy thereof; in any court of law within the British colonies and plantations in America, a stamp duty of three pence.

For every skin or piece of vellum or parchment, or sheet or piece of paper, on which shall be engrossed, written, or printed, any special bail, and appearance upon such bail in any such court, a stamp duty of two shillings.

For every skin or piece of vellum or parchment, or sheet or piece of paper, on which may be engrossed, written, or printed, any petition, bill, answer, claim, plea, replication, rejoinder, demurrer, or other pleading, in any court of chancery or equity within the said colonies and plantations, a stamp duty of one shilling and six pence.

For every skin or piece of vellum or parchment, or sheet or piece of paper, on which shall be engrossed, written, or printed, any copy of any position, bill, answer, claim, plea, replication, rejoinder, demurrer, or other pleading in any such court, a stamp duty of three pence.

For every skin or piece of vellum or parchment, or sheet or piece of paper, on which shall be engrossed, written, or printed, any monition, libel, answer, allegation, inventory, or renunciation in ecclesiastical matters, in any court of probate court of the ordinary, or other court exercising ecclesiastical jurisdiction within the said colonies and plantations, a stamp duty of one shilling.

For every skin or piece of vellum or parchment, or sheet or piece of paper, on which shall be engrossed, written, or printed, any copy of any will (other than the probate thereof) monition, libel, answer, allegation, inventory, or renunciation in ecclesiastical matters, in any such court, a stamp duty of six pence.

For every skin or piece of vellum or parchment, or sheet or piece of paper, on which shall be engrossed, written, or printed, any donation, presentation, collation or institution, of or to any benefice, or any writ or instrument for the like purpose, or any register, entry, testimonial, or certificate of any degree taken in any university, academy, college, or seminary of learning within the said colonies and plantations, a stamp duty of two pounds.

For every skin or piece of vellum or parchment, or sheet or piece of paper, on which shall be engrossed, written, or printed, any monition, libel, claim, answer, allegation, information, letter of request, execution, renunciation, inventory, or other pleading, in any admiralty court, within the said colonies and plantations, a stamp duty of one shilling.

For every skin or piece of vellum or parchment, or sheet or piece of paper, on which any copy of any such monition, libel, claim, answer, allegation, information, letter of request, execution, renunciation, inventory, or other pleading shall be engrossed, written, or printed, a stamp duty of six pence.

For every skin or piece of vellum or parchment, or sheet or piece of paper, on which shall be engrossed, written, or printed, any appeal, writ of error, writ of dower, ad quod damnum, certiorari, statute merchant, statute staple, attestation, or certificate, by any officer, or exemplification of any record or proceeding, in any court whatsoever, within the said colonies and plantations (except appeals, writs of error, certiorari attestations, certificates, and exemplifications, for, or relating to the removal of any proceedings from before a single justice of the peace), a stamp duty of ten shillings.

For every skin or piece of vellum or parchment, or sheet or piece of paper, on which shall be engrossed, written, or printed, any writ of covenant for levying fines, writ of entry for suffering a common recovery, or attachment issuing out of, or returnable into, any court within the said colonies and plantations, a stamp duty of five shillings.

For every skin or piece of vellum or parchment, or sheet or piece of paper, on which shall be engrossed, written, or printed, any judgment, decree, sentence, or dismission or any record of nisi prius or postea, in any court within the said colonies and plantations, a stamp duty of four shillings.

For every skin or piece of vellum or parchment, or sheet or piece of paper, on which shall be engrossed, written, or printed, any affidavit, common bail, or appearance, interrogatory, deposition, rule, order or warrant of any court, or any dedimus potestatem, capias subpoena, summons, compulsory citation, commission, recognizance, or any other writ, process, or mandate, issuing out of, or returnable into, any court, or any office belonging thereto, or any other proceeding therein whatsoever, or any copy thereof, or of any record not herein before charged, within the said colonies and plantations (except warrants relating to criminal matters, and proceedings thereon, or relating thereto), a stamp duty of one shilling.

For every skin or piece of vellum or parchment, or sheet or piece of paper, on which shall be engrossed, written, or printed, any note or bill of lading, which shall be signed for any kind of goods, wares, or merchandise, to be exported from, or any cocket or clearance granted within the said colonies and plantations, a stamp duty of four pence.

For every skin or piece of vellum or parchment, or sheet or piece of paper, on which shall be engrossed, written, or printed, letters of mart or commission for private ships of war, within the said colonies and plantations, a stamp duty of twenty shillings.

For every skin or piece of vellum or parchment, or sheet or piece of paper, on which shall be engrossed, written, or printed, any grant, appointment, or admission of, or to, any public beneficial office or employment, for the space of one year, or any lesser time, of or above twenty pounds per annum sterling money, in salary, fees, and perquisites, within the said colonies and plantations (except commissions and appointments of officers of the army, navy, ordnance, or militia, of judges, and of justices of the peace), a stamp duty of ten shillings.

For every skin or piece of vellum or parchment, or sheet or piece of paper, on which any grant, of any liberty, privilege, or franchise, under the seal or sign manual of any governor, proprietor, or public officer, alone, or in conjunction with any other person or persons, or with any council, or any council and assembly, or any exemplification of the same, shall be engrossed, written, or printed, within the said colonies and plantations, a stamp duty of six pounds.

For every skin or piece of vellum or parchment, or sheet or piece of paper, on which shall be engrossed, written, or printed, any license for retailing of spirituous liquors, to be granted to any person who shall take out the same, within the said colonies and plantations, a stamp duty of twenty shillings.

For every skin or piece of vellum or parchment, or sheet or piece of paper, on which shall be engrossed, written, or printed, any license for retailing of wine, to be granted to any person who shall not take out a license for retailing of spirituous liquors, within the said colonies and plantations, a stamp duty of four pounds.

For every skin or piece of vellum or parchment, or sheet or piece of paper, on which shall be engrossed, written, or printed, any license for retailing of wine, to be granted to any person who shall take out a license for retailing of spirituous liquors, within the said colonies and plantations, a stamp duty of three pounds.

For every skin or piece of vellum or parchment, or sheet or piece of paper, on which shall be engrossed, written, or printed, any probate of will, letters of administration, or of guardianship for any estate above the value of twenty pounds sterling money, within the British colonies and plantations upon the continent of America, the islands belonging thereto and the Bermuda and Bahama islands, a stamp duty of five shillings.

For every skin or piece of vellum or parchment, or sheet or piece of paper, on which shall be engrossed, written, or printed, any such probate, letters of administration or of guardianship, within all other parts of the British dominions in America, a stamp duty of ten shillings.

For every skin or piece of vellum or parchment, or sheet or piece of paper, on which shall be engrossed, written, or printed, any bond for securing the payment of any sum of money, not exceeding the sum of ten pounds sterling money within the British colonies and plantations upon the continent of America, the islands belonging thereto, and the Bermuda and Bahama islands, a stamp duty of six pence.

For every skin or piece of vellum or parchment, or sheet or piece of paper, on which shall be engrossed, written, or printed, any bond for securing the payment of any sum of money above ten pounds, and not exceeding twenty pounds sterling money, within such colonies, plantations, and islands a stamp duty of one shilling.

For every skin or piece of vellum or parchment, or sheet or piece of paper, on which shall be engrossed, written, or printed, any bond for securing the payment of any sum of money above twenty pounds, arid not exceeding forty pounds sterling money, within such colonies, plantations, and islands, a stamp duty of one shilling and six pence.

For every skin or piece of vellum or parchment, or sheet or piece of paper, on which shall be engrossed, written, or printed, any order or warrant for surveying or setting out any quantity of land, not exceeding one hundred acres, issued by any governor, proprietor, or any public officer, alone, or in conjunction with any other person or persons, or with any council, or any council and assembly, within the British colonies and plantations in America, a stamp duty of six pence.

For every skin or piece of vellum or parchment, or sheet or piece of paper, on which shall be engrossed, written, or printed, any such order or warrant for surveying or setting out any quantity of land above one hundred and not exceeding two hundred acres, within the said colonies and plantations, a stamp duty of one shilling.

For every skin or piece of vellum or parchment, or sheet or piece of paper, on which shall be engrossed, written, or printed, any such order or warrant for surveying or setting out any quantity of land above two hundred, and not exceeding three hundred and twenty acres, and in proportion for every such order or warrant for surveying or setting out every other three hundred and twenty acres, within the said colonies and plantations, a stamp duty of one shilling and six pence.

For every skin or piece of vellum or parchment, or sheet or piece of paper, on which shall be engrossed, written, or printed, any original grant, or any deed, mesne conveyance, or other instrument whatsoever, by which any quantity of land, not exceeding one hundred acres, shall be granted, conveyed, or assigned, within the British colonies and plantations upon the continent of America, the islands belonging thereto, and the Bermuda and Bahama islands (except leases for any term not exceeding the term of twenty one years), a stamp duty of one shilling and six pence.

For every skin or piece of vellum or parchment, or sheet or piece of paper, on which shall be engrossed, written, or printed, any such original grant, or any such deed, mesne conveyance, or other instrument whatsoever, by which any quantify of land above one hundred, and not exceeding two hundred acres, shall be granted, conveyed, or assigned, within such colonies, plantations, and islands, a stamp duty of two shillings.

For every skin or piece of vellum or parchment, or sheet or piece of paper, on which shall be engrossed, written, or printed, any such original grant, or any such deed, mesne conveyance, or other instrument whatsoever, by which any quantity of land above two hundred, and not exceeding three hundred and twenty acres, shall be granted, conveyed, or assigned, and in proportion for every such grant, deed, mesne conveyance, or other instrument, granting, conveying, or assigning, every other three hundred and twenty acres, within such colonies, plantations, and islands, a stamp duty of two shillings and six pence.

For every skin or piece of vellum or parchment, or sheet or piece of paper, on which shall be engrossed, written, or printed, any such original grant, or any such deed, mesne conveyance, or other instrument whatsoever, by which any quantity of land, not exceeding one hundred acres, stall be granted, conveyed, or assigned, within all other parts of the British dominions in America, a stamp duty of three shillings.

For every skin or piece of vellum or parchment, or sheet or piece of paper, on which shall be engrossed, written, or printed, any such original grant, or any such deed, mesne conveyance, or other instrument whatsoever, by which any quantity of land above one hundred, and not exceeding two hundred acres, shall be granted, conveyed, or assigned, within the same parts of the said dominions, a stamp duty of four shillings.

For every skin or piece of vellum or parchment, or sheet or piece of paper, on which shall be engrossed, written, or printed, any such original grant, or any such deed, mesne conveyance, or other instrument whatsoever, by which any quantity of land above two hundred, and not exceeding three hundred twenty acres, shall he granted, conveyed, or assigned, and in proportion for every such grant, deed, mesne conveyance, or other instrument, granting, conveying, or assigning every other three hundred and twenty acres, within the same parts of the said dominions, a stamp duty of five shillings.

For every skin or piece of vellum or parchment, or sheet or piece of paper, on which shall be engrossed, written, or printed, any grant, appointment, or admission, of or to any beneficial office or employment, not herein before charged, above the value of twenty pounds per annum sterling money in salary, fees, and perquisites, or any exemplification of the same, within the British colonies and plantations upon the continent of America, the islands belonging thereto, and the Bermuda and Bahama islands (except commissions of officers of the army, navy, ordnance, or militia, and of justices of the pence), a stamp duty of four pounds.

For every skin or piece of vellum or parchment, or sheet or piece of paper, on which shall be engrossed, written, or printed, any such grant, appointment, or admission, of or to any such public beneficial office or employments or any exemplification of the same, within all other parts of the British dominions in America, a stamp duty of six pounds.

For every skin or piece of vellum or parchment, or sheet or piece of paper, on which shall be engrossed, written, or printed, any indenture, lease, conveyance, contract, stipulation, bill of sale, charter party, protest, articles of apprenticeship or covenant (except for the hire of servants not apprentices, and also except such other matters as herein before charged) within the British colonies and plantations in America, a stamp duty of two shillings and six pence.

For every skin or piece of vellum or parchment, or sheet or piece of paper, on which any warrant or order for auditing any public accounts, beneficial warrant, order grant, or certificate, under any public seal, or under the send or sign manual of any governor, proprietor, or public officer, alone, or in conjunction with any person or persons, or with any council, or any council and assembly, not herein before charged, or any passport or let pass, surrender of office, or policy of assurance, shall be engrossed, written, or printed, within the said colonies and plantations (except warrants or orders for the service of the army, navy, ordnance, or militia, and grants of offices under twenty pounds per annum, in salary, fees, and perquisites), a stamp duty of five shillings.

For every skin or piece of vellum or parchment, or sheet or piece of paper, on which shall be engrossed, written or printed, any notarial net, bond, deed, letter of attorney, procuration, mortgage, release, or other obligatory instrument, not herein before charged, within the said colonies and plantations, a stamp duty of two shillings and three pence.

For every skin or piece of vellum or parchment, or sheet or piece of paper, on which shall be engrossed, written, or printed, any register, entry, or enrollment of any grant, deed or other instrument whatsoever, herein before charged, within the said colonies and plantations, a stamp duty of three pence.

For every skin or piece of vellum or parchment, or sheet or piece of paper, on which shall be engrossed, written, or printed, any register, entry, or enrollment of any grant, deed, or other instrument whatsoever, not herein before charged, within the said colonies and plantations, a stamp duty of two shillings.

And for and upon every pack of playing cards, and all dice, which shall be sold or used within the said colonies and plantations, the several stamp duties following (that is to say):

For every pack of such cards, one shilling.

And for every pair of such dice, ten shillings.

And for and every paper called a pamphlet, and upon every newspaper, containing public news or occurrences, which shall be printed, dispersed, and made public, within any of the said colonies and plantations, and for and upon such advertisements as are hereinafter mentioned, the respective duties following (that is to say):

For every such pamphlet and paper contained in a half sheet, or any lesser piece of paper, which shall be so printed, a stamp duty of one half penny for every printed copy thereof.

For every such pamphlet and paper (being larger than half a sheet, and not exceeding one whole sheet), which shall be printed, a stamp duty of one penny for every printed copy thereof.

For every pamphlet and paper, being larger than one whole sheet, and not exceeding six sheets in octavo, or in a lesser page, or not exceeding twelve sheets in quarto, or twenty sheets in folio, which shall be so printed, a duty after the rate of one shilling for every sheet of any kind of paper which shall be contained in one printed copy thereof.

For every advertisement to be contained in any gazette newspaper, or other paper, or any pamphlet which shall be so printed, a duty of two shillings.

For every almanac, or calendar, for any one particular year, or for any time less than a year, which shall be written or printed on one side only of any one sheet, skin, or piece of paper, parchment, or vellum, within the said colonies and plantations, a stamp duty of two pence.

For every other almanac or calendar, for any one particular year, which shall be written or printed within the said colonies and plantations, a stamp duty of four pence.

And for every almanac or calendar, written or printed in the said colonies and plantations, to serve for several years, duties to the same amount respectively shall be paid for every such year.

For every skin or piece of vellum or parchment, or sheet or piece of paper, on which any instrument, proceeding, or other matter or thing aforesaid, shall be engrossed, written, or printed, within the said colonies and plantations, in any other than the English language, a stamp duty of double the amount of the respective duties before charged thereon.

And there shall be also paid, in the said colonies and plantations, a duty of six pence for every twenty shillings, in any sum not exceeding fifty pounds sterling money, which shall be given, paid, contracted, or agreed for, with, or in relation to, any clerk or apprentice, which shall be put or placed to or with any master or mistress, to learn any profession, trade, or employment.

II

And also a duty of one shilling for every twenty shillings, in any sum exceeding fifty pounds, which shall be given, paid, contracted, or agreed for, with, or in relation to, any such clerk or apprentice...

V

And be it further enacted ..., That all books and pamphlets serving chiefly for the purpose of an almanack, by whatsoever name or names intituled or described, are and shall be charged with the duty imposed by this act on almanacks, but not with any of the duties charged by this act on pamphlets, or other printed papers ...

VI

Provided always, that this act shall not extend to charge any bills of exchange, accompts, bills of parcels, bills of fees, or any bills or notes not sealed for payment of money at sight, or upon demand, or at the end of certain days of payment....

XII

And be it further enacted ..., That the said several duties shall be under the management of the commissioners, for the time being, of the duties charged on stamped vellum, parchment, and paper, in Great Britain: and the said commissioners are hereby impowered and required to employ such officers under them, for that purpose, as they shall think proper....

XVI

And be it further enacted... That no matter or thing whatsoever, by this act charged with the payment of a duty, shall be pleaded or given in evidence, or admitted in any court within the said colonies and plantations, to be good, useful, or available in law or equity, unless the same shall be marked or stamped, in pursuance of this act, with the respective duty hereby charged thereon, or with an higher duty....

LIV

And be it further enacted ... That all the monies which shall arise by the several rates and duties hereby granted (except the necessary charges of raising, collecting, recovering, answering, paying, and accounting for the same and the necessary charges from time to time incurred in relation to this act, and the execution thereof) shall be paid into the receipt of his Majesty's exchequer, and shall be entered separate and apart from all other monies, and shall be there reserved to be from time to time disposed of by parliament, towards further defraying the necessary expenses of defending, protecting, and securing, the said colonies and plantations....

LVII

... offenses committed against any other act or acts of Parliament relating to the trade or revenues of the said colonies or plantations; shall and may be prosecuted, sued for, and recovered, in any court of record, or in any court of admiralty, in the respective colony or plantation where the offense shall be committed, or in any court of vice admiralty appointed or to be appointed, and which shall have jurisdiction within such colony, plantation, or place, (which courts of admiralty or vice admiralty are hereby respectively authorized and required to proceed, hear, and determine the same) at the election of the informer or prosecutor.....

The Townshend Acts (June-July 1767)

The British Parliament

"Nervous tension" is the term that best describes the relationship between the American colonies and England in the aftermath of the Stamp Act repeal.

Several issues remained unresolved. First, Parliament had absolutely no wish to send a message across the Atlantic that ultimate authority lay in the colonial legislatures. Immediately after repealing the Stamp Act, Parliament issued the Declaratory Act.

This act proclaimed Parliament's ability "to bind the colonies in all cases whatsoever." The message was clear: under no circumstances did Parliament abandon in principle its right to legislate for the 13 colonies.

In the Western Hemisphere, leaders were optimistic about the repeal of the Stamp Act but found the suggestions of the Declaratory Act threatening. Most American statesmen had drawn a clear line between legislation and taxation. In 1766, the notion of Parliamentary supremacy over the law was questioned only by a radical few, but the ability to tax without representation was another matter. The DECLARATORY ACT made no such distinction. "All cases whatsoever" could surely mean the power to tax. Many assemblymen waited anxiously for the issue to resurface.

From infancy I was taught to love humanity and liberty. Inquiry and experience have since confirmed my reverence for the lessons then given me by convincing me more fully of their truth and excellence. Benevolence toward mankind excites wishes for their welfare, and such wishes endear the means of fulfilling them. These can be found in liberty only, and therefore her sacred cause ought to be espoused by every man, on every occasion, to the utmost of his power. As a charitable but poor person does not withhold his mite because he cannot relieve all the distresses of the miserable, so should not any honest man suppress his sentiments concerning freedom, however small their influence is likely to be. Perhaps he may "touch some wheel" that will have an effect greater than he could reasonably expect...

– John Dickinson, Letters from a Farmer in Pennsylvania to the Inhabitants of the British Colonies (1767)

Boston Non-Importation Agreement

August 1, 1768

The merchants and traders in the town of Boston having taken into consideration the deplorable situation of the trade, and the many difficulties it at present labours under on account of the scarcity of money, which is daily increasing for want of the other remittances to discharge our debts in Great Britain, and the large sums collected by the officers of the customs for duties on goods imported; the heavy taxes levied to discharge the debts contracted by the government in the late war; the embarrassments and restrictions laid on trade by several late acts of parliament; together with the bad success of our cod fishery, by which our principal sources of remittance are like to be greatly diminished, and we thereby rendered unable to pay the debts we owe the merchants in Great Britain, and to continue the importation of goods from thence;

We, the subscribers, in order to relieve the trade under those discouragements, to promote industry, frugality, and economy, and to discourage luxury, and every kind of extravagance, do promise and engage to and with each other as follows:

First, That we will not send for or import from Great Britain, either upon our own account, or upon commission, thisfall, any other goods than what are already ordered for the fall supply.

Secondly, That we will not send for or import any kind of goods or merchandize from Great Britain, either on our own account, or on commissions, or any otherwise, from the 1st of January 1769, to the 1st of January 1770, except salt, coals, fish hooks and lines, hemp, and duck bar lead and shot, woolcards and card wire.

Thirdly, That we will not purchase of any factor, or others, any kind of goods imported from Great Britain, from January 1769, to January 1770.

Fourthly, That we will not import, on our own account, or on commissions or purchase of any who shall import from any other colony in America, from January 1769, to January 17 70, any tea, glass, paper, or other goods commonly imported from Great Britain.

Fifthly, That we will not, from and after the 1st of January 1769, import into this province any tea, paper, glass, or painters colours, until the act imposing duties on those articles shall be repealed.

In witness whereof, we have hereunto set our hands, this first day of August, 1768.

The Boston Massacre (March 1770)

The Boston Massacre

The Boston Massacre was a street fight that occurred on March 5, 1770, between a "patriot" mob, throwing snowballs, stones, and sticks, and a squad of British soldiers. Several colonists were killed and this led to a campaign by speech-writers to rouse the ire of the citizenry.

The presence of British troops in the city of Boston was increasingly unwelcome. The riot began when about 50 citizens attacked a British sentinel. A British officer, Captain Thomas Preston, called in additional soldiers, and these too were attacked, so the soldiers fired into the mob, killing 3 on the spot (a black sailor named Crispus Attucks, ropemaker Samuel Gray, and a mariner named James Caldwell), and wounding 8 others, two of whom died later (Samuel Maverick and Patrick Carr).

A town meeting was called demanding the removal of the British and the trial of Captain Preston and his men for murder. At the trial, John Adams and Josiah Quincy II defended the British, leading to their acquittal and release. Samuel Quincy and Robert Treat Paine were the attorneys for the prosecution. Later, two of the British soldiers were found guilty of manslaughter.

The Boston Massacre was a signal event leading to the Revolutionary War. It led directly to the Royal Governor evacuating the occupying army from the town of Boston. It would soon bring the revolution to armed rebellion throughout the colonies.

Note that the occupation of Boston by British troops in 1768 was not met by open resistance.

The Boston Tea Party (December 1773)

Boston Tea Party

Governor THOMAS HUTCHINSON allowed three ships carrying tea to enter Boston Harbor. Before the tax could be collected, Bostonians took action. On a cold December night, radical townspeople stormed the ships and tossed 342 chests of tea into the water. Disguised as Native Americans, the offenders could not be identified.

I dressed myself in the costume of an Indian,equipped with a small hatchet, which I and my associates denominated the tomahawk, with which, and a club, after having painted my face and hands with coal dust in the shopof a blacksmith, I repaired to Griffin's wharf,where the ships lay that contained the tea...

We then were ordered by our commander to open the hatches and take out all the chests of tea and throw them overboard, and we immediately proceeded to execute his orders, first cutting and splitting the chests with our tomahawks, so as thoroughly to expose them to the effects of the water. In about three hours from the time we went on board, we had thus broken and thrown overboard every tea chest to be found in the ship, while those in the other ships were disposing of the tea in the same way, at the same time. We were surrounded by British armed ships, but no attempt was made to resist us.

– Anonymous, "Account of the Boston Tea Party by a Participant," (1773)

The damage in modern American dollars exceeded three quarters of a million dollars. Not a single British East India Company chest of tea bound for the 13 colonies reached its destination. Not a single American colonist had a cup of that tea.

Only the fish in Boston Harbor had that pleasure.

<u>The Intollerable (March-June 1774)</u>

The Upper House Of Parliament

Someone was going to pay.

Parliament was utterly fed up with colonial antics. The British could tolerate strongly worded letters or trade boycotts. They could put up with defiant legislatures and harassed customs officials to an extent.

But they saw the destruction of 342 chests of tea belonging to the British East India Company as wanton destruction of property by Boston thugs who did not even have the courage to admit responsibility.

Someone was going to pay.

Calami-tea

The British called their responsive measures to the Boston Tea Party the COERCIVE ACTS. Boston Harbor was closed to trade until the owners of the tea were compensated. Only food and firewood were permitted into the port. Town meetings were banned, and the authority of the royal governor was increased.

To add insult to injury, General Gage, the British commander of North American forces, was appointed governor of Massachusetts. British troops and officials would now be tried outside Massachusetts for crimes of murder. Greater freedom was granted to British officers who wished to house their soldiers in private dwellings.

This Town has received the Copy of an Act of the British Parliament, wherein it appears that we have been tried and condemned, and are to be punished, by the shutting up of the harbor and other marks of revenge, until we shall disgrace ourselves by servilely yielding up, in effect, the just and righteous claims of America....The people receive this cruel edict with abhorrence and indignation. They consider themselves as suffering the stroke ministerial...I hope they will sustain the blow with a becoming fortitude, and that the cursed design of intimidating and subduing the spirits of all America, will, by the joint efforts of all, be frustrated.

– Samuel Adams, letter to James Warren (May 14, 1774)

The Quebec Act

Parliament seemed to have a penchant for bad timing in these years. Right after passing the Coercive Acts, it passed the QUEBEC ACT, a law that recognized the Roman Catholic Church as the established church in Quebec. An appointed council, rather than an elected body, would make the major decisions for the colony. The boundary of Quebec was extended into the Ohio Valley.

In the wake of the passage of the Quebec Act, rage spread through the 13 colonies. With this one act, the British Crown granted land to the French in Quebec that was clearly desired by the American colonists. The extension of tolerance to Catholics was viewed as a hostile act by predominantly Protestant America.

Democracy took another blow with the establishment of direct rule in Quebec. Although the British made no connection between the Coercive Acts and the Quebec Act, they were seen on the American mainland as malicious deed and collectively called the INTOLERABLE ACTS.

INTOLERABLE ACTS

Boston Port Act:-An act to discontinue, in such manner, and for or such time as are therein mentioned, the landing and discharging, lading or shipping, of goods, wares, and merchandise, at the town, and within the harbour, of Boston, in the province of Massachusetts Bay, in North America.

Massachusetts Government Act:- An Act for the better regulating the government of the province of the Massachusetts Bay in New England.

Administration of Justice Act:- An act for the impartial administration of justice in the case of persons questioned for any acts done by them in the execution of the law, or for the suppression of riots and tumults, in the province of the Massachusetts Bay, in New England.

Quebec Act:- An Act for making effectual Provision for the Government of the Province of Quebec in North America.

Throughout the colonies, the message was clear: what could happen in Massachusetts could happen anywhere. The British had gone too far. Supplies were sent to the beleaguered colony from the other twelve. For the first time since the Stamp Act Crisis, an intercolonial conference was called.

It was under these tense circumstances that the FIRST CONTINENTAL CONGRESS convened in Philadelphia on September 5, 1774.

Lexington and Concord (April 1775)

Britain's General Gage had a secret plan.

During the wee hours of April 19, 1775, he would send out regiments of British soldiers quartered in Boston. Their destinations were LEXINGTON, where they would capture Colonial leaders Sam Adams and John Hancock, then CONCORD, where they would seize gunpowder.

But spies and friends of the Americans leaked word of Gage's plan.

Two lanterns hanging from Boston's North Church informed the countryside that the British were going to attack by sea. A series of horseback riders — men such as Paul Revere, WILLIAM DAWES and DR. SAMUEL PRESCOTT — galloped off to warn the countryside that the REGULARS (British troops) were coming.

We set off for Concord, and were overtaken by a young gentleman named Prescot, who belonged to Concord, and was going home. When we had got about half way from Lexington to Concord, the other two stopped at a house to awake the men, I kept along ....

In an instant I saw four of them, who rode up to me with their pistols in their bands, said "G---d d---n you, stop. If you go an inch further, you are a dead man." Immediately Mr. Prescot came up. We attempted to get through them, but they kept before us, and swore if we did not turn in to that pasture, they would blow our brains out, (they had placed themselves opposite to a pair of bars, and had taken the bars down). They forced us in. When we had got in, Mr. Prescot said "Put on!" He took to the left, I to the right ...

Just as I reached it, out started six officers, seized my bridle, put their pistols to my breast, ordered me to dismount, which I did.

– Paul Revere, "Account of Midnight Ride to Lexington" (1775)

Word spread from town to town, and militias prepared to confront the British and help their neighbors in Lexington and Concord.

These COLONIAL MILITIAS had originally been organized to defend settlers from civil unrest and attacks by French or Native

Americans. Selected members of the militia were called MINUTEMEN because they could be ready to fight in a minute's time.

Sure enough, when the advance guard of nearly 240 British soldiers arrived in Lexington, they found about 70 minutemen formed on the LEXINGTON GREEN awaiting them. Both sides eyed each other warily, not knowing what to expect. Suddenly, a bullet buzzed through the morning air.

It was "the shot heard round the world."

Concord

The numerically superior British killed seven Americans on Lexington Green and marched off to Concord with new regiments who had joined them. But American militias arriving at Concord thwarted the British advance.

As the British retreated toward Boston, new waves of Colonial militia intercepted them. Shooting from behind fences and trees, the militias inflicted over 125 casualties, including several officers. The ferocity of the encounter surprised both sides.

Lt. Col. Smith's Report to Gen. Gage

In obedience to your Excellency's commands, I marched on the evening of the 18th inst. with the corps of grenadiers and light infantry for Concord, to execute your Excellency's orders with respect to destroying all ammunition, artillery, tents, &c., collected there, which was effected, having knocked off the trunnions of three pieces of iron ordnance, some new gun carriages, a great number of carriage wheels burnt, a considerable quantity of flour, some gunpowder and musket balls, with other small articles thrown into the river. Notwithstanding we marched with the utmost expedition and secrecy, we found the country had intelligence or strong suspicion of our coming, and fired many signal guns, and rung the alarm bells repeatedly; and were informed, when at Concord, that some cannon had been taken out of the town that day, that others, with some stores, had been carried three days before ....

I think it proper to observe, that when I had got some miles on the march from Boston, I detached six light infantry companies to march with all expedition to seize the two bridges on different roads beyond Concord. On these companies' arrival at Lexington, I understand, from the report of Major Pitcairn, who was with them, and from many officers, that they found on a green close to the road a body of the country people drawn up in military order, with arms and accoutrements, and, as appeared after, loaded; and that they had posted some men in a dwelling and Meeting-house. Our troops advanced towards them, without any intention of injuring them, further than to inquire the reason of their being thus assembled, and, if not satisfactory, to have secured their arms; but they in confusion went off, principally to the left, only one of them fired before he went off, and three or four more jumped over a wall and fired from behind it among the soldiers; on which the troops returned it, and killed several of them. They likewise fired on the soldiers from the Meeting and dwelling-house. We had one man wounded, and Major Pitcairn's horse shot in two places. Rather earlier than this, on the road, a country man from behind a wall had snapped his piece at Lieutenants Adair and Sutherland, but it flashed and did not go off. After this we saw some in the woods, but marched on to Concord without anything further happening. While at Concord we saw vast numbers assembling in many parts; at one of the bridges they marched down, with a very considerable body, on the light infantry posted there. On their coming pretty near, one of our men fired on them, which they returned; on which an action ensued, and some few were killed and wounded. In this affair, it appears that after the bridge was quitted, they scalped and otherwise ill-treated one or two of the men who were either killed or severely wounded, being seen by a party that marched by soon after. At Concord we found very few inhabitants in the town; those we met with both Major Pitcairn and myself took all possible pains to convince that we meant them no injury, and that if they opened their doors when required to search for military stores, not the slightest mischief would be done. We had opportunities of convincing them of our good intentions, but they were sulky; and one of them even struck Major Pitcairn. On our leaving Concord to return to Boston, they began to fire on us from behind the walls, ditches, trees, etc., which, as we marched, increased to a very great degree, and continued without the intermission of five minutes altogether, for, I believe, upwards of eighteen miles; so that I can't think but it must have been a preconcerted scheme in them, to attack the King's troops the first favourable opportunity that offered, otherwise, I think they could not, in so short a time as from our marching out, have raised such a numerous body, and for so great a space of ground. Notwithstanding the enemy's numbers, they did not make one gallant effort during so long an action, though our men were so very much fatigued, but kept under cover.

– Lieutenant Colonel Smith, 10th Regiment of Foot, letter to General Gage (April 22, 1775)

The first bloodshed at Lexington and Concord, marked the crossing of a threshold, and the momentum from these events pushed both sides farther apart. Following the battles, neither the British nor the Americans knew what to expect next.

Indignation against the British ran high in the Colonies — for they had shed American blood on American soil. Radicals such as Sam Adams took advantage of the bloodshed to increase tensions through propaganda and rumor-spreading. The Americans surrounded the town of Boston, and the rebel army started gaining many new recruits.

During the battles of Lexington and Concord, 73 British soldiers had been killed and 174 wounded; 26 were missing. LORD PERCY, who led the British back into Boston after the defeat suffered at Concord, wrote back to London, "Whoever looks upon them [THE REBELS] as an irregular mob will be much mistaken." Three British major generals — WILLIAM HOWE, HENRY CLINTON, and "GENTLEMAN JOHNNY" BURGOYNE — were brought to Boston to lend their expertise and experience to the situation.

Benedict Arnold and Ethan Allen Join the Cause

Shortly after the battle, an express rider carried the news to New Haven, Connecticut, where a local militia commander and wealthy shopkeeper named Benedict Arnold demanded the keys to a local powder house.

After arming himself and paying money from his own pocket to outfit a group of militia from Massachusetts, Arnold and his men set off for upstate New York. He was searching for artillery that was badly needed for the Colonial effort and reckoned that he could commandeer some cannon by capturing Fort Ticonderoga, a rotting relic from the French and Indian War.

Up in the HAMPSHIRE GRANTS, part of modern-day Vermont, ETHAN ALLEN who led a group called the GREEN MOUNTAIN BOYS, also had the idea to capture Fort Ticonderoga. The two reluctantly worked together and surprised the poorly manned British fort before dawn on May 10, 1775.

The fort's commander had been asleep and surrendered in his pajamas!

British attacks on coastal towns (October 1775-January 1776)

British raids on American coastal towns in late 1775 also contributed to a general deterioration of relations between Great Britain and her American colonies. On October 18, 1775, the British Navy bombarded and burned the town of Falmouth, Massachusetts (known today as Portland, Maine).

CHAPTER FOUR

Course Of The Revolution

March 22, 1765: Stamp Act

Like the Sugar Act (1764), the Stamp Act was imposed to provide increased revenues to meet the costs of defending the enlarged British Empire. It was the first British parliamentary attempt to raise revenue through direct taxation on a wide variety of colonial transactions, including legal writs, newspaper advertisements, and ships' bills of lading. Enraged colonists nullified the Stamp Act through outright refusal to use the stamps as well as by riots, stamp burning, and intimidation of colonial stamp distributors.

June 15–July 2, 1767: Townshend Acts

A series of four acts, the Townshend Acts were passed by the British Parliament in an attempt to assert what it considered to be its historic right to exert authority over the colonies through suspension of a recalcitrant representative assembly and through strict provisions for the collection of revenue duties. The acts were resisted everywhere with verbal agitation and physical violence, deliberate evasion of duties, renewed nonimportation agreements among merchants, and overt acts of hostility toward British enforcement agents, especially in Boston. In response, in October 1768, Parliament dispatched two regiments of the British army to Boston.

March 5, 1770: Boston Massacre

In Boston, a small British army detachment that was threatened by mob harassment opened fire and killed five people, an incident soon known as the Boston Massacre. The soldiers were charged with murder and were given a civilian trial, in which John Adams conducted a successful defense.

December 16, 1773: Boston Tea Party

Protesting both a tax on tea (taxation without representation) and the perceived monopoly of the East India Company, a party of Bostonians thinly disguised as Mohawk people boarded ships at anchor and dumped some £10,000 worth of tea into the harbor, an event popularly known as the Boston Tea Party.

March–June 1774: Intolerable Acts

In retaliation for colonial resistance to British rule during the winter of 1773–74, the British Parliament enacted four measures that became known as the Intolerable (or Coercive) Acts: the Boston Port Act, Massachusetts Government Act, Administration of Justice Act, and Quartering Act. Rather than intimidating Massachusetts and isolating it from the other colonies, the oppressive acts became the justification for convening the First Continental Congress later in 1774.

September 5, 1774: First Continental Congress convenes

Called by the Committees of Correspondence in response to the Intolerable Acts, the First Continental Congress convened in Philadelphia. Fifty-six delegates represented all the colonies except Georgia.

March 23, 1775: Patrick Henry's "Give me liberty or give me death" speech

Convinced that war with Great Britain was inevitable, Virginian Patrick Henry defended strong resolutions for equipping the Virginia militia to fight against the British in a fiery speech in a Richmond church with the famous words, "I know not what course others may take, but as for me, give me liberty or give me death!"

April 18–19, 1775: Paul Revere's Ride and the Battles of Lexington and Concord

On the night of April 18, 1775, Paul Revere rode from Charlestown to Lexington (both in Massachusetts) to warn that the British were marching from Boston to seize the colonial armory at Concord. En route, the British force of 700 men was met on Lexington Green by 77 local minutemen and others. It is unclear who fired the first shot, but it sparked a skirmish that left eight Americans dead. At Concord, the British were met by hundreds of militiamen. Outnumbered and running low on ammunition, the British column was forced to retire to Boston. On the return march, American snipers took a deadly toll on the British. Total losses in the Battles of Lexington and Concord numbered 273 British and more than 90 Americans.

June 17, 1775: Battle of Bunker Hill

Breed's Hill in Charlestown was the primary locus of combat in the misleadingly named Battle of Bunker Hill, which was part of the American siege of British-held Boston. Some 2,300 British troops eventually cleared the hill of the entrenched Americans, but at the cost of more than 40 percent of the assault force. The battle was a moral victory for the Americans.

January 1776: Thomas Paine's Common Sense published

In late 1775 the colonial conflict with the British still looked like a civil war, not a war aiming to separate nations; however, the publication of Thomas Paine's irreverent pamphlet Common Sense abruptly put independence on the agenda. Paine's 50-page pamphlet, couched in elegant direct language, sold more than 100,000 copies within a few months. More than any other single publication, Common Sense paved the way for the Declaration of Independence.

July 4, 1776: Declaration of Independence adopted

After the Congress recommended that colonies form their own governments, the Declaration of Independence was written by Thomas Jefferson and revised in committee. On July 2 the Congress voted for independence; on July 4 it adopted the Declaration of Independence.

September 22, 1776: Nathan Hale executed

On September 21, 1776, having penetrated the British lines on Long Island to obtain information, American Capt. Nathan Hale was captured by the British. He was hanged without trial the next day. Before his death, Hale is thought to have said, "I only regret that I have but one life to lose for my country," a remark similar to one in the play Cato by Joseph Addison.

December 25–26, 1776: Washington crosses the Delaware

Having been forced to abandon New York City and driven across New Jersey by the British, George Washington and the Continental Army struck back on Christmas night by stealthily crossing the ice-strewn Delaware River, surprising the Hessian garrison at Trenton at dawn, and taking some 900 prisoners. The American triumph at Trenton and in the Battle of Princeton (January 3, 1777) roused the new country and kept the struggle for independence alive.

October 17, 1777: Burgoyne surrenders at Saratoga

Moving south from Canada in summer 1777, a British force under Gen. John Burgoyne captured Fort Ticonderoga (July 5) before losing decisively at Bennington, Vermont (August 16), and Bemis Heights, New York (October 7). His forces depleted, Burgoyne surrendered at Saratoga.

December 19, 1777–June 19, 1778: Washington winters at Valley Forge

Following failures at the Battles of Brandywine and Germantown, Washington and 11,000 regulars took up winter quarters at Valley Forge, 22 miles (35 km) northwest of British-occupied Philadelphia. Although its ranks were decimated by rampant disease, semi-starvation, and bitter cold, the reorganized Continental Army emerged the following June as a well-disciplined and efficient fighting force.

February 6, 1778: France and the United States form an alliance

The French had secretly furnished financial and material aid to the Americans since 1776, but with the signing in Paris of the Treaty of Amity and Commerce and the Treaty of Alliance, the Franco-American alliance was formalized. France began preparing fleets and armies to enter the fight but did not formally declare war on Britain until June 1778.

September 23, 1779: John Paul Jones: "I have not yet begun to fight!"

The U.S. battleship the Bonhomme Richard was getting the worst of its battle with the British vessel HMS Serapis off Flamborough Head, England, when the American commander, John Paul Jones, refused to surrender, proclaiming, "I have not yet begun to fight!" Jones ultimately triumphed, but he lost his ship in the process.

September 1780: Benedict Arnold turns traitor

Having fought valiantly in a number of battles earlier in the war, American Gen. Benedict Arnold conspired with the British to surrender the fort at West Point, New York, that he commanded. When John André, the British army officer with whom Arnold had negotiated, was hanged as a spy after he was captured and the plot revealed, Arnold took sanctuary with the British.

March 1, 1781: Articles of Confederation ratified

The Articles of Confederation, a plan of government organization that served as a bridge between the initial government by the Continental Congress and the federal government provided under the U.S. Constitution of 1787, were written in 1776–77 and adopted by the Congress on November 15, 1777. However, the articles were not fully ratified by the states until March 1, 1781.

September–October 1781: Siege of Yorktown

After winning a costly victory at Guilford Courthouse, North Carolina, on March 15, 1781, Lord Cornwallis entered Virginia to join other British forces there, setting up a base at Yorktown. Washington's army and a force under the French Count de

Rochambeau placed Yorktown under siege, and Cornwallis surrendered his army of more than 7,000 men on October 19, 1781.

September 3, 1783: Treaty of Paris ends the war

After the British defeat at Yorktown, the land battles in America largely died out—but the fighting continued at sea, chiefly between the British and America's European allies, which came to include Spain and the Netherlands. The military verdict in North America was reflected in the preliminary Anglo-American peace treaty of 1782, which was included in the Treaty of Paris of 1783. By its terms, Britain recognized the independence of the United States with generous boundaries, including the Mississippi River on the west. Britain retained Canada but ceded East and West Florida to Spain.

Impact Of American Revolution

The Bill Of American Rights

1. REPUBLICAN GOVERNMENTS

The American Revolution led to genuinely democratic politics becoming possible in the former colonies. In fact, the most important immediate consequence of America declaring independence was the creation of written state constitutions in 1776 and 1777. These new state constitutions were based on the idea of "popular sovereignty", that is, the power and authority of the government derived from the people. A declaration or "bill" of rights was incorporated in many of these constitutions to protect the rights of individuals. Moreover, concepts of liberty, equality among men and hostility toward corruption became incorporated as core values of liberal republicanism. The new state constitutions often extended the franchise to adopt universal male suffrage with no property qualifications. Along with the new constitutions, there was a reform in penal code which eliminated such brutal physical punishments as ear-cropping and branding, all still widely practiced in Britain.

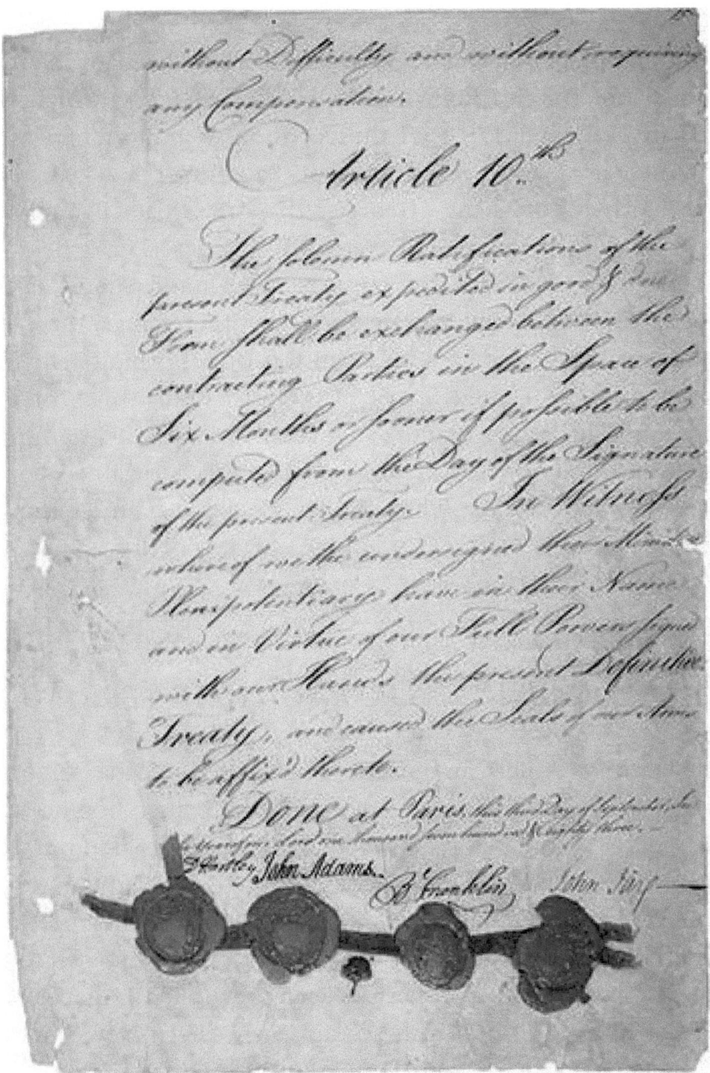

Treaty Of Paris

2 INDEPENDENCE OF THE UNITED STATES

The American Revolutionary War was officially brought to an end with a set of treaties known as the Peace of Paris, which were signed in 1783 and 1784. Of these, the most important was the Treaty of Paris, which was signed on September 3, 1783 by the representatives of King George III of Great Britain and representatives of the United States of America. The article 1 of this treaty acknowledged the existence of United States' as free, sovereign and independent states. Among other things, the Treaty of Paris set the boundaries between the British Empire in North America and the United States of America. The Peace of Paris also resulted in France gaining two small colonies, Tobago in the West Indies and Senegal in West Africa; Spain regained control of Menorca and Florida; while the Dutch didn't gain anything of significant value.

3 NATIVE AMERICANS LOSING THEIR TERRITORY

Several Native American groups participated in the American Revolution. Majority of them sided with the British hoping that a British victory would stop continued colonial expansion into their territories. However, most didn't directly participate in the war and remained neutral seeing little value in joining what they perceived to be a European conflict. The Mohawk chief Thayendanegea was one of the major Native American leaders who led Indian, British and Loyalist forces on punishing raids in western New York and Pennsylvania in 1778 and 1779. After the war, the peace negotiations had no native representatives. The British granted the United States all land between the Appalachian Mountains and the Mississippi River even though this region was largely unsettled by whites and mostly inhabited by Native Americans. Soon after gaining independence, the United States rapidly expanded westward, often brutally, acquiring Indian lands by treaty and by force. Stockbridges and Oneidas who had supported the Americans lost lands as well as Senecas and Shawnees who had fought against them. It may be said that American independence marked the beginning of the end of what had remained of Native American independence.

4 LOYALIST EXPATRIATION

When the American revolution started, the population in the colonies was divided into the Patriots, the ones who supported the revolution; and the Loyalists, those Americans who remained faithful to the British Empire during the war. Around 20% of the population of the colonies were Loyalists. However, a small percentage of them actively supported the British cause. During the Revolution, the Loyalists had to suffer regular harassment for supporting the Crown. When the United States gained independence, an estimated 60,000 to 100,000 Loyalists left the newly found nation. Of these, some migrated to Britain. However, a great majority received land and subsidies for resettlement in British colonies in what now is Canada, especially Quebec, Prince Edward Island and Nova Scotia. Nonetheless, around 85% of the Loyalists stayed in the United States as American citizens and some who had left also returned at a later date

5 REPUBLICAN MOTHERHOOD

Although the American Revolution did not have a revolutionary impact in the lives of women in the United States, there were some important changes. Republicanism was the driving ideology of the revolution and this in turn led to a concept known as "Republican Motherhood". A successful republic rested on the virtue of its citizens and, for that to happen, the role of the mother became paramount. It was believed that daughters in a family needed to be raised to uphold the ideals of republicanism so that, when they became mothers, they could pass on republican values to the next generation. Though it limited the role of a woman to the domestic sphere, Republican Motherhood encouraged the education of women. Despite this, American women still found themselves subordinated, legally and socially, to their husbands, disfranchised and usually with only the role of mother open to them. Nonetheless, the education of women had a long term influence as educated women would begin the women's rights movement in the United States by mid-19th century.

6 ECONOMIC IMPACT

The American Revolutionary War put an immense strain on the economy of the United States. After gaining independence, the new national government owed approximately $12 million in foreign debt and $44 million in domestic debt; and state governments owed approximately $25 million, mostly in war debts. Moreover, the new currency had an enormous inflation rate and deprecated dramatically. However, at the same time, the Revolution ended the various restrictions imposed by the British on the colonial economies including limiting trade, settlement and manufacturing. Thus new markets were opened and new trade relationships were established. The was perhaps the most important economic consequence of the Revolution for America in the long term. The United States would go on to recover from the economic challenges posed by the Revolution and enter into two centuries of unprecedented growth which would make it the leading economy in the world

8 IMPACT ON THE BRITISH EMPIRE

Apart from losing an important part of their Empire, Great Britain lost a huge amount of money in fighting the American Revolutionary War. This led to the national debt soaring and creating a yearly interest of nearly 10 million pounds. As a result, taxes had to be raised. Moreover, imports and exports experienced large drops and the following recession caused stocks and land prices to plummet. At the same time, the level of unemployment fell as Britain needed more men for the army and trade with U.S. rose to the same level as trade with the colonies by 1785. The American Revolution also led to the British Empire employing two distinct forms of imperialism: one for native people and the other for European settlers. While the Britishers continued to oppress native people in Asia and Africa, they increasingly accommodated settler demands for autonomy and self-government in their white colonies. In 1791, Quebec was divided into two colonies, Upper and Lower Canada, each with its own elected assembly. In Australia, agitation for representative government resulted in the Australian Colonies Government Act of 1850; while New Zealand got a representative government in 1852.

CHAPTER SIX

What Was American Civil War

The American Civil War was a civil war in the United States between the Union and the Confederacy. The central cause of the war was the status of slavery, especially the expansion of slavery into territories acquired as a result of the Louisiana Purchase and the Mexican–American War.

CHAPTER SEVEN

Causes Of American Civil War

The Civil War is the central event in America's historical consciousness. While the Revolution of 1776-1783 created the United States, the Civil War of 1861-1865 determined what kind of nation it would be. The war resolved two fundamental questions left unresolved by the revolution: whether the United States was to be a dissolvable confederation of sovereign states or an indivisible nation with a sovereign national government; and whether this nation, born of a declaration that all men were created with an equal right to liberty, would continue to exist as the largest slaveholding country in the world.

Northern victory in the war preserved the United States as one nation and ended the institution of slavery that had divided the country from its beginning. But these achievements came at the cost of 625,000 lives--nearly as many American soldiers as died in all the other wars in which this country has fought combined. The American Civil War was the largest and most destructive conflict in the Western world between the end of the Napoleonic Wars in 1815 and the onset of World War I in 1914.

Abraham Lincoln

There were not many causes for the starting of American Civil War :-

The Civil War started because of uncompromising differences between the free and slave states over the power of the national government to prohibit slavery in the territories that had not yet become states. When Abraham Lincoln won election in 1860 as the first Republican president on a platform pledging to keep slavery out of the territories, seven slave states in the deep South seceded and formed a new nation, the Confederate States of America. The incoming Lincoln administration and most of the Northern people refused to recognize the legitimacy of secession. They feared that it would discredit democracy and create a fatal precedent that would eventually fragment the no-longer United States into several small, squabbling countries.

The event that triggered war came at Fort Sumter in Charleston Bay on April 12, 1861. Claiming this United States fort as their own, the Confederate army on that day opened fire on the federal garrison and forced it to lower the American flag in surrender. Lincoln called out the militia to suppress this "insurrection." Four more slave states seceded and joined the Confederacy. By the end of 1861 nearly a million armed men confronted each other along a line stretching 1200 miles from Virginia to Missouri. Several battles had already taken place--near Manassas Junction in Virginia, in the mountains of western Virginia where Union victories paved the way for creation of the new state of West Virginia, at Wilson's Creek in Missouri, at Cape Hatteras in North Carolina, and at Port Royal in South Carolina where the Union navy established a base for a blockade to shut off the Confederacy's access to the outside world.

But the real fighting began in 1862. Huge battles like Shiloh in Tennessee, Gaines' Mill, Second Manassas, and Fredericksburg in Virginia, and Antietam in Maryland foreshadowed even bigger campaigns and battles in subsequent years, from Gettysburg in Pennsylvania to Vicksburg on the Mississippi to Chickamauga and Atlanta in Georgia. By 1864 the original Northern goal of a limited war to restore the Union had given way to a new strategy of "total war" to destroy the Old South and its basic institution of slavery and to give the restored Union a "new birth of freedom," as President Lincoln put it in his address at Gettysburg to dedicate a cemetery for Union soldiers killed in the battle there.

Alexander Gardner's famous photo of Confederate dead before the Dunker Church on the Antietam Battlefield in Sharpsburg, Md., 1862.

For three long years, from 1862 to 1865, Robert E. Lee's Army of Northern Virginia staved off invasions and attacks by the Union Army of the Potomac commanded by a series of ineffective generals until Ulysses S. Grant came to Virginia from the Western theater to become general in chief of all Union armies in 1864. After bloody battles at places with names like The Wilderness, Spotsylvania, Cold Harbor, and Petersburg, Grant finally brought Lee to bay at

Appomattox in April 1865. In the meantime Union armies and river fleets in the theater of war comprising the slave states west of the Appalachian Mountain chain won a long series of victories over Confederate armies commanded by hapless or unlucky Confederate generals. In 1864-1865 General William Tecumseh Sherman led his army deep into the Confederate heartland of Georgia and South Carolina, destroying their economic infrastructure while General George Thomas virtually destroyed the Confederacy's Army of Tennessee at the battle of Nashville.

By the spring of 1865 all the principal Confederate armies surrendered, and when Union cavalry captured the fleeing Confederate President Jefferson Davis in Georgia on May 10, 1865, resistance collapsed and the war ended. The long, painful process of rebuilding a united nation free of slavery began.

CHAPTER EIGHT

Abraham Lincoln

Abraham Lincoln (/ˈlɪŋkən/; February 12, 1809 – April 15, 1865) was an American lawyer and statesman who served as the 16th president of the United States from 1861 until his assassination in 1865. Lincoln led the nation through the American Civil War and succeeded in preserving the Union, abolishing slavery, bolstering the federal government, and modernizing the U.S. economy.

Lincoln was born into poverty in a log cabin in Kentucky and was raised on the frontier, primarily in Indiana. He was self-educated and became a lawyer, Whig Party leader, Illinois state legislator, and U.S. Congressman from Illinois. In 1849, he returned to his law practice but became vexed by the opening of additional lands to slavery as a result of the Kansas–Nebraska Act of 1854. He reentered politics in 1854, becoming a leader in the new Republican Party, and he reached a national audience in the 1858 Senate campaign debates against Stephen Douglas. Lincoln ran for President in 1860, sweeping the North to gain victory. Pro-slavery elements in the South viewed his election as a threat to slavery, and Southern states began seceding from the Union. During this time the newly formed Confederate States of America began seizing federal military bases in the south. Just over one month after Lincoln assumed the presidency, the Confederate States attacked Fort Sumter, a U.S. fort in South Carolina. Following the bombardment, Lincoln mobilized forces to suppress the rebellion and restore the Union.

Lincoln, a moderate Republican, had to navigate a contentious array of factions with friends and opponents from both the Democratic and Republican parties. His allies, the War Democrats and the Radical Republicans, demanded harsh treatment of the Southern Confederates. Anti-war Democrats (called "Copperheads") despised Lincoln, and irreconcilable pro-Confederate elements plotted his assassination. He managed the factions by exploiting their mutual enmity, carefully distributing political patronage, and by appealing to the American people. His Gettysburg Address appealed to nationalistic, republican, egalitarian, libertarian, and democratic sentiments. Lincoln closely supervised the strategy and tactics in the war effort, including the selection of generals, and implemented a naval blockade of the South's trade. He suspended habeas corpus in Maryland, and he averted British intervention by defusing the Trent Affair. In 1863 he issued the Emancipation Proclamation, which declared the slaves in the states "in rebellion" to be free. It also directed the Army and Navy to "recognize and maintain the freedom of such persons" and to receive them "into the armed service of the United States." Lincoln also pressured border states to outlaw slavery, and he promoted the Thirteenth Amendment to the United States Constitution, which upon its ratification abolished slavery.

Lincoln managed his own successful re-election campaign. He sought to heal the war-torn nation through reconciliation. On April 14, 1865, just days after the war's end at Appomattox, he was attending a play at Ford's Theatre in Washington, D.C., with his wife Mary when he was fatally shot by Confederate sympathizer John Wilkes Booth. Abraham Lincoln is remembered as a martyr and a national hero for his wartime leadership and for his efforts to preserve the Union and abolish slavery. Lincoln is often ranked by both popular and scholarly polls as the greatest president in American history.

Abraham Lincoln

CHAPTER NINE

Role Of Abraham Lincoln in Civil War

Lincoln warned the South in his Inaugural Address: "In your hands, my dissatisfied fellow countrymen, and not in mine, is the momentous issue of civil war. The government will not assail you.... You have no oath registered in Heaven to destroy the government, while I shall have the most solemn one to preserve, protect and defend it."

Lincoln thought secession illegal, and was willing to use force to defend Federal law and the Union. When Confederate batteries fired on Fort Sumter and forced its surrender, he called on the states for 75,000 volunteers. Four more slave states joined the Confederacy but four remained within the Union. The Civil War had begun.

The son of a Kentucky frontiersman, Lincoln had to struggle for a living and for learning. Five months before receiving his party's nomination for President, he sketched his life:

"I was born Feb. 12, 1809, in Hardin County, Kentucky. My parents were both born in Virginia, of undistinguished families–second families, perhaps I should say. My mother, who died in my tenth year, was of a family of the name of Hanks.... My father ... removed from Kentucky to ... Indiana, in my eighth year.... It was a wild region, with many bears and other wild animals still in the woods. There I grew up.... Of course when I came of age I did not know much. Still somehow, I could read, write, and cipher ... but that was all."

Lincoln made extraordinary efforts to attain knowledge while working on a farm, splitting rails for fences, and keeping store at New Salem, Illinois. He was a captain in the Black Hawk War, spent eight years in the Illinois legislature, and rode the circuit of courts for many years. His law partner said of him, "His ambition was a little engine that knew no rest."

He married Mary Todd, and they had four boys, only one of whom lived to maturity. In 1858 Lincoln ran against Stephen A. Douglas for Senator. He lost the election, but in debating with Douglas he gained a national reputation that won him the Republican nomination for President in 1860.

As President, he built the Republican Party into a strong national organization. Further, he rallied most of the northern Democrats to the Union cause. On January 1, 1863, he issued the Emancipation Proclamation that declared forever free those slaves within the Confederacy.

Lincoln never let the world forget that the Civil War involved an even larger issue. This he stated most movingly in dedicating the military cemetery at Gettysburg: "that we here highly resolve that these dead shall not have died in vain—that this nation, under God, shall have a new birth of freedom—and that government of the people, by the people, for the people, shall not perish from the earth."

Lincoln won re-election in 1864, as Union military triumphs heralded an end to the war. In his planning for peace, the President was flexible and generous, encouraging Southerners to lay down their arms and join speedily in reunion.

The spirit that guided him was clearly that of his Second Inaugural Address, now inscribed on one wall of the Lincoln Memorial in Washington, D. C.: "With malice toward none; with charity for all; with firmness in the right, as God gives us to see the right, let us strive on to finish the work we are in; to bind up the nation's wounds.... "

On Good Friday, April 14, 1865, Lincoln was assassinated at Ford's Theatre in Washington by John Wilkes Booth, an actor, who somehow thought he was helping the South. The opposite was the result, for with Lincoln's death, the possibility of peace with magnanimity died.

The Presidential biographies on WhiteHouse.gov are from "The Presidents of the United States of America," by Frank Freidel and Hugh Sidey. Copyright 2006 by the White House Historical Association.

CHAPTER TEN

Effects Of Civil War

There were many effects of American civil war

1 EMANCIPATION PROCLAMATION

Although Abraham Lincoln considered slavery as an abhorrent evil, as a lawyer and a politician he knew that the constitution protected slavery in the states where the citizens seemed to want it. In his first inaugural address, Lincoln declared that he had "no purpose, directly or indirectly, to interfere with slavery in the States where it exists". With his election as president, the Secession Crisis and the Civil War, the political scenario began to change. After a series of victories in the early 1862, the Union suffered some demoralizing defeats. The large slave population of the south, though not involved in direct action, were helping the southerners in various other ways. The argument that emancipation was a military necessity was gaining ground. In mid-1862, Lincoln decided on the Emancipation Proclamation calling his cabinet for discussion. However, Lincoln's Secretary of State William H. Seward persuaded him to withhold the proclamation as the Union armies were being defeated. Seward argued that the sudden move would look like an act of desperation.

On September 17, 1862 the Union forces forced the Confederates to retreat at the Battle of Antietam. A tactical and moral victory for the North rather than a military one. Five days later on 22nd September, 1862 Lincoln issued a preliminary warning that he would order the emancipation of all slaves in any state that did not end its rebellion against the Union by January 1, 1863. The proclamation came into effect on the historic day of January 1, 1863 legally freeing 3.1 million of the nation's 4 million slaves. It is noteworthy that the new law did not free slaves being held in the border states of Delaware, Maryland, Kentucky and Missouri. Lincoln was concerned that the issuance of a universal emancipation of all slaves would persuade these states to secede from the Union and join the Confederacy.

2 DIVISION OF VIRGINIA

On April 17, 1861, the Richmond convention of Virginia voted on the Ordinance of Secession to secede from the Union. But many delegates hailing from the western counties of Virginia were opposed to the idea. Almost immediately after the adoption of the ordinance, a meeting of such delegates look place at Clarksburg recommending that each county in north western Virginia send delegates to a convention to meet in Wheeling. This led to three conventions at Wheeling in May, June and July of 1861 and formation of the "Restored Government of Virginia" which gave legitimacy to the formation of one state within another. This meant that there was a point when there were two governments claiming to represent all of Virginia, one owing allegiance to the United States and one to the Confederacy. The politics continued for the next few months. Finally President Lincoln approved the formation of West Virginia in 1862 which officially became a state on June 20, 1863, the only state to form by seceding from a Confederate state.

3 BIGGEST LOSS OF LIFE IN U.S. HISTORY

The American Civil War remains the deadliest battle for the country with estimated deaths between 600,000 and 800,000. The war claimed close to 50 percent more American lives than World War 2, and 5 to 6 times more lives than World War 1. The Battle of Gettysburg was the bloodiest of all claiming close to 50,000 casualties followed by Chickamauga and Spotsylvania. Diseases, infections and injury were the giant killers. Wounded soldiers were housed in overfilled hospitals with filthy conditions. The worst injuries were caused by the Minni Ball rifle bullets of British Enfield and American Springfield rifles, which were used extensively in the war. Conditions were deplorable in Union and Confederate prisons, where prisoners often died from outright neglect or starvation. At the infamous Camp Sumter prison camp in Georgia, prisoners were described as "walking skeletons". The Camp Sumter prison claimed the life of close to a fourth of its 45,000 prisoners.

4 CONSTITUTIONAL AMENDMENTS AND CHANGE IN DEFINITION OF AMERICAN CITIZENSHIP

In the five years immediately following the Civil War the United States constitution adopted the 13th, 14th and the 15th Constitutional amendments between 1865 and 1870. These amendments were added more than 60 years after the 12th amendment of 1804 and primarily dealt with the issue of African Americans, people of color and slavery. The amendments are also called the Reconstruction Amendments as they were important in the reconstruction of Southern America after the Civil War.

The Thirteenth Amendment to the United States Constitution officially abolished slavery and involuntary servitude, except as punishment for a crime. The US senate passed it on 8th April, 1864 and it was incorporated into the federal constitution on 18th December, 1865.

The Fourteenth Amendment was bitterly contested especially by the Southern States. Added to the Federal Constitution on July 20, 1868, the amendment declared that all persons born or naturalized in the United States are American citizens including African Americans.

The Fifteenth Amendment prohibited the federal and state governments from denying a citizen the right to vote based on that citizen's "race, color, or previous condition of servitude". It was ratified and added to the Federal Constitution on February 3, 1870.

Fortieth Congress of the United States of America;

At the *First* Session.

Begun and held at the city of Washington, on Monday, the *seventh* day of *December*, one thousand eight hundred and sixty-eight.

A RESOLUTION

Proposing an amendment to the Constitution of the United States.

Resolved by the Senate and House of Representatives of the United States of America in Congress assembled, (two-thirds of both Houses concurring) That the following article be proposed to the Legislatures of the several States as an amendment to the Constitution of the United States, which, when ratified by three-fourths of said Legislatures shall be valid as part of the Constitution, namely:

Article XV.

Section 1. The right of citizens of the United States to vote shall not be denied or abridged by the United States or by any State on account of race, color, or previous condition of servitude.—

Section 2. The Congress shall have power to enforce this article by appropriate legislation.—

Schuyler Colfax
Speaker of the House of Representatives.

B. F. Wade
President of the Senate pro tempore.

Attest:
Edw. McPherson
Clerk of House of Representatives.

Geo. C. Gorham
Secy. of Senate U.S.

The Amendment

5 ASSASSINATION OF ABRAHAM LINCOLN

After the surrender of Robert E Lee to Ulysses Grant at Appomattox Court on 9th April, 1865, the Civil War was at its dusk. John Wilkes Booth was a native of Maryland who had remained in the North during the Civil War. He was a prominent stage actor and Confederate sympathizer who viewed Abraham Lincoln as a tyrant. With his initial plan of abducting Abraham Lincoln failing on 20th March 1865 and Confederate General Lee surrendering a few weeks later, Booth become desperate. Learning that Lincoln was to attend Laura Keene's acclaimed performance of "Our American Cousin" at Ford's Theatre in Washington, D.C. he hatched a sinister plan to kill three prominent Union leaders and throw the government into disarray. At 10:15 PM on the 14th of April 1885, John Wilkes Booth slipped into the box where Lincoln was seated and fired his .44-caliber single-shot derringer pistol into the back of Lincoln's head. He then escaped after jumping on the stage. The other acts of the plot failed as Lewis Powell failed to kill Secretary of State William H. Seward and George Atzerodt failed to attack Vice President Andrew Johnson. Unwilling to surrender, Booth was shot dead on 26th April. His co-conspirators were convicted for their part in the assassination and executed by hanging on July 7, 1865.

Assassination Of Abraham Lincoln

6 RECONSTRUCTION ACTS OF 1867-68

After the end of the civil war there were many debates about how the former Confederate states would re-join the Union. In a way, there was an attempt at the transformation of the 11 Confederate States that had seceded from the Union. Abraham Lincoln had proposed lenient Reconstruction policies and, after his assassination, new president Andrew Jackson intended to follow the same principle. But the more radical Republicans and powerful anti-slavery groups were committed to equal rights for freed blacks and favored more stringent action. It was these groups that were majorly responsible for crafting the Reconstruction Acts. The first bill divided 10 rebel states into five military districts for governance and they were required to draft new constitutions that would be approved by the US Congress. Three more acts were passed in

1867-68 which were concerned about how the new constitutions would be created and passed at the state level.

7 THE POLITICS AND VIOLENCE OF RECONSTRUCTION ERA

The Reconstruction Era refers to the period immediately following the American Civil War from 1865 (the end of the Confederacy) to 1877. The south was in disarray after the war and was still not part of the Union. Many bills and laws were passed during the reconstruction era with the aim of reintegrating the South into the Federal structure. The Republican Party gained in prominence and the period changed the southern society and culture in many ways. Among other things, there was a rise of violence and riots against the black communities and formation of many racist groups like the Red Shirts in Mississippi and the Carolinas, and the White League in Louisiana. Most of the violence was however carried out by members of the Ku Klux Klan (KKK), a secretive terrorist organization closely allied with the southern Democratic Party.

The 1866 Election gave the Republicans majority in Congress and enabled them to pass the 14th Amendment, upgrading the rights of African Americans and curtailing the powers of ex-confederates. Civil war veteran and radical republican Ulysses S Grant was elected as President in 1868. He strengthened Washington's legal capabilities to directly intervene to protect citizenship rights of African Americans and crushed any acts of violence against them. However, in the 1876 presidential election, Republican nominee Rutherford Hayes negotiated with southern political leaders to get elected. The federal troops returned in 1877 marking the end of the Reconstruction Era.

In the coming years new racial systems would disenfranchise black voters and they would remain tied to low wage employment in agriculture and households. Thus Reconstruction is generally viewed as a failure. However, the seed of the Reconstruction Era would remain planted in the constitution bearing fruit over close to 100 years later in the Civil Rights Movement, sometimes also called the "Second Reconstruction".

8 SCALAWAGS AND CARPETBAGGERS

The defeat of the South led to the breakdown of its economic, social and political situation as was known before the war. Most Confederate military and political leaders were temporarily prohibited from participating in the political process which led to the creation of a vacuum. This further led to the emergence of two groups that were called Scalawags and Carpetbaggers in a derogatory sense. Scalawags, which meant worthless livestock, referred to native white Southerners who supported the federal reconstruction plan and cooperated with the blacks. The majority of them were small non slave-holding farmers, merchants and other professionals who had remained loyal to the Union during the civil war. Although viewed as traitors in the South, the Scalawags made up close to 20 percent of the white electorate and wielded considerable influence especially after the civil war. The term Carpetbagger referred to a poor traveler who arrives with only a carpetbag and slowly fills up his bag by exploiting his surrounding conditions. The term was used to describe the white Northerners who, motivated by profit or idealism, moved to the south after the Civil War. Many carpetbaggers were from the educated middle class of various walks of life. They saw themselves as reformers and wanted to shape the post war South in the image of the North. Carpetbaggers were hated by the southerners as low-class and opportunistic newcomers seeking to get rich on their misfortune.

9 THE JIM CROW LAWS

After the end of the reconstruction period in 1877, as the white southerners began gaining power again, methods were developed to bypass the Reconstruction laws and subjugate the black people. The people who did this called themselves Redeemers. They aimed at taking away the civil rights of the blacks by twisting existing laws and bringing in new ones. The laws came to be known as Jim Crow Laws, named after a racist cartoon strip of a poor uneducated black man. The laws ranged from being inhuman like forcing black people to sit in the back of public buses to insane such as a requiring black people to "qualify" to vote by paying poll taxes, or, by reciting the entire Declaration of Independence or Constitution from memory or the one where official records of black births, marriages, and deaths could not be kept in the same books that contained records of white births, marriages, and deaths. The Jim Crow Laws continued to be enforced until 1965, when they were ultimately overruled by the Civil Rights Act of 1964 and the Voting Rights Act of 1965.

10 THE RISE OF INDUSTRIALISM

Before the Civil War the Southern economy was largely agricultural, dependent on cotton and other cash crops while the North was more industrialized. The political tensions between the two had led to years of policy paralysis. The North was forced to delay and compromise on their economic objectives due to strong Southern opposition and their political and economic clout. With the secession of the southern states the northerners began implementing their way of thought through various laws and acts such as the Morrill Tariff of 1861, which increased import tariff in the U.S. to foster rapid industrial growth; and the Transcontinental Railroad Acts, that provided federal subsidies in land and loans for the construction of a transcontinental railroad across the U.S. These measures, including many others, would provide impetus to the industrial growth of the United States. Industrialization, in turn, led to the creation of massive corporations and companies and the emergence of the entrepreneurs.

Printed by Libri Plureos GmbH in Hamburg,
Germany